Rainforests are thick forests that get a lot of rain. They are hot and wet.

Not all the rainforests have been explored yet.

The biggest rainforest is the Amazon in South America.

There are lots of different trees in the rainforests.

trees

Hundreds of different animals live in the rainforests.

A rainforest has different levels.

Parrots swoop about in the thick tree tops.

Some animals that live in the tree tops never come to the forest floor.

Small tree frogs live in pools in the tree tops.

tree frog

On the ground it is hot, dark, and gloomy. The trees have big roots to help them stand up.

Insects live here, and there are all sorts of ferns and mushrooms.

Loggers cut the trees and sell the wood, and the land is farmed for food.

The rainforests are vanishing.

We must help stop this happening!